IDEA
CATCHER

AN INSPIRING
JOURNAL
FOR WRITERS

FROM THE EDITORS OF STORY PRESS

STORY PRESS
CINCINNATI, OHIO

CONTENTS

IDEA CATCHERS

For the notions, observations, schemes, dreams and visions,
we'd like to thank the following idea catchers:

Greg Albert	Anne Hevener
Jennie Berliant	Kirsten Holm
Peter Blocksom	Marc Jennings
William Brohaugh	Jennifer Lepore
Ted Cains	April Lindner
Katie Carroll	Paul Mandelbaum
Thomas Clark	David Nielson
John Drury	Lois Rosenthal
Mark Garvey	Angela Terez
Robin Gee	David Tompkins
Jack Heffron	Bruce Woods
Laurie Henry	Meredith Wolf

INTRODUCTION

The writing life is as thrilling as a ride on a roller coaster but just as fraught with dips and peaks. Blank pages can be a blessing or a nemesis depending on whether work is moving along or you are stuck in a slump.

To help keep words flowing, we created *Idea Catcher*, a journal divided into seven sections to organize and record what you hear or overhear, what you think and feel and remember. For instance, if the person ahead of you in the supermarket checkout line strikes you as wonderfully eccentric because of the conglomeration of food you notice in her cart, remember to flip to the "People and Characters" section and jot down your observations. What kind of person pairs caviar and Fritos? Does she eat alone? Let your mind whir. Then when you're stumped for a character, flip to that section and your inspiration is right where you left it.

In *Idea Catcher*, you'll also find exercises to help get you started if you've hit a dry spell. Here's an example. "Imagine you are a tiny pebble being churned into a piece of sand by the ocean. Describe how it feels." We've also found quotes from famous writers to inspire you, as well as anecdotes about how great work was born, often from a single image or a snatch of conversation. For example, you'll learn what compelled John Steinbeck to write *The Grapes of Wrath*, his novel that changed the course of history. Why not you?

The goal of this journal is to help you catch ideas. We hope it becomes your private place to dream and create, a place where no thought is too silly or slight or strange. Take risks. Every time you open *Idea Catcher*, a new adventure begins.

—The Editors of Story Press

IDEAS

Turn into your favorite car. Are you a Jaguar? A Jeep? What does it feel like?

Read a letter to "Dear Abby" or "Ann Landers," but ignore the reply. Write a piece that centers on or even resolves the conflict that provoked the letter.

Think about a secret you've kept—about yourself. Give the mystery to a character unlike you.

"There are significant moments in everyone's day that can make literature. That's what you ought to write about." —Raymond Carver

Revise a fairy tale, using the villain's point of view. For example, the witch might have had good reasons for cooking Hansel and Gretel or the big bad wolf for wanting to eat the three little pigs.

Find an interesting photograph in a magazine. Disregard the caption and write your own version of what's happening in the picture.

On the way to work you see a car run a red light and nearly cause a fatal accident. What could have been on the driver's mind?

William Faulkner was inspired to write his great novel "The Sound and the Fury" by a glimpse of a little girl perched in a tree and wearing muddy underwear. The girl was leaning toward an open second-floor window, apparently eavesdropping. He began to imagine, then to write about, the conversation the girl was overhearing.

Go to a courtroom and watch a few trials. Write about an intriguing case from the point of view of one of the participants.

Author James M. Cain once wrote, "I write of the wish that comes true—for some reason, a terrifying thought." Recall an unfulfilled wish of your own. How would your life have changed if the wish had come true?

Choose an event from today's world news—an earthquake, a revolution, a famine—and imagine it taking place in your own community.

"For any writer who wants to keep a journal, be alive to everything, not just to what you're feeling, but also to your pets, to flowers, to what you're reading."

—May Sarton

Look for stories in your everyday life. How, for instance, did the middle-aged man with the operatic voice wind up working the counter at your local deli?

Read your horoscope. Record your day as if the prediction came true.

Compare someone you once loved to the animal he or she most resembled. Write a short piece in which the person is magically turned into that animal.

"One of the obligations of the writer is to say or sing all that he or she can, to deal with as much of the world as becomes possible to him or her in language."

—Denise Levertov

You are a comic book superhero or supervillain. What powers do you possess? What does your costume look like? What is your goal—to save the world? To rule it?

Remember something funny that happened to you, then write about it in a bittersweet way so that people may laugh—or cry.

Find a "must sell" ad in the classified section of your newspaper. Imagine the situation fueling the urgency.

"Somebody gets into trouble, gets out of it again. People love that story. They never get tired of it." —Kurt Vonnegut

Have you ever seen a ghost, heard something strange in the night? Describe this unexplainable, even supernatural, experience, and be convincing enough to make it seem real.

Write a love letter you'd never dare send.

Recall where you were when a historical event occurred—the Kennedy assassination, V-J Day, the explosion of the Challenger space shuttle. How did you feel when you heard the news? What does it mean to you now?

Meld the characteristics of five different animals to create a new type of creature. What does it look like? How does it behave? Unleash this beast and describe what happens.

"If you are a writer you locate yourself behind a wall of silence and no matter what you are doing, driving a car or walking or doing housework...you can still be writing, because you have that space."   —Joyce Carol Oates

Write a letter congratulating yourself on something you did especially well today.

Find a tragic story in the newspaper and create a happy ending.

Write about a beautiful place you've visited from the point of view of someone who doesn't appreciate the splendor. He might find the Bahamas too hot, Rome too dirty, the pyramids less majestic than they look in pictures.

Tennessee Williams began his famous play "A Streetcar Named Desire" from a mental image of a woman sitting alone by a window and looking very sad from having been stood up by the man she was supposed to marry. This image evolved into the character of Blanche DuBois, who brings her heartache to New Orleans and ignites the action of the play.

What risk do you regret not taking—anything from turning down a marriage proposal to chickening out on the ten-foot-high diving board? Take that chance now, on paper. What happens?

Wait for a full moon. Spread a beach towel and take a moonbath.
How does it make you feel?

Go to a secondhand store and pick out something that interests you—a vintage mantle clock, a tweed jacket, a set of old dishes—and invent the object's original owners.

"Any writer overwhelmingly honest about pleasing himself is almost sure to please others."

—Marianne Moore

PEOPLE AND CHARACTERS

What was Hamlet like as a child? Or Scarlett O'Hara? Invent the life of a favorite character as it occurred before the time of the story.

Who is the "black sheep" of your family? Make this person so admirable that readers will like, even respect, him.

"I write because I want more than one life; I insist on a wider selection. It's greed plain and simple. When my characters join the circus, I'm joining the circus."

—Anne Tyler

The first human lands on Mars. She steps out of the spacecraft and says....

As you wait in the supermarket checkout line, pay attention to the people in front of you. Write a few paragraphs about someone who catches your eye.

Choose an imaginary figure from your childhood—Santa Claus, the Tooth Fairy, the Sandman—and give him or her a darker, more realistic side. Is the Sandman an insomniac? The Tooth Fairy a kleptomaniac?

While looking out her window one winter day, Eudora Welty saw an old black woman hobbling along in the distance. Welty wondered where she could be going in such cold weather. She decided that the woman was on a mission of mercy, an errand, perhaps, for a family member. She then began to write her classic short story "A Worn Path," in which old Phoenix Jackson journeys to get medicine for her sick grandson.

A man has been murdered while he worked late one night. There are five suspects. Explain from each suspect's point of view why he or she didn't commit the crime.

Drive to an unfamiliar part of your town and choose a house that appeals to you. Write about who might live there, using details about the house and its surroundings to develop the characters.

Describe—with great fondness—a person you love, but focus on some aspect of their appearance or behavior that a stranger might not find so lovable, such as your son's adorable tendency to draw on the wallpaper, your spouse's endearing double chin.

"When I'm writing, I'm waiting to see somebody, and I'm waiting to hear them. It's almost like conjuring spirits out of the air, using your own imaginative instability." —Charles Baxter

Mix and match personality traits of real people in your life. An uncle's gambling addiction could be paired with your brother's religious obsessions. Throw in your father's need for an evening walk and develop this new character.

Write a letter to an old friend. Discuss an issue that has bothered you for a long time.

Find a tree or picnic table with initials or names carved into it, proclaiming true love. A wall of graffiti will do. Bring this relationship to life. Who are these people? Are they really so in love? <u>Both</u> of them?

Characters sometimes point the way. Anne Rice was working on a story about vampires but found herself blocked, unsure where the story should go. Then she wrote, "'Do you want to hold the interview here?' asked the vampire." That voice and that question led her to complete the story, which she later developed into her best-selling novel "Interview With the Vampire."

Portray a character by describing the belongings in her wallet, desk drawers, kitchen cabinets, car trunk, you name it.

List a few traits that you admire in people, such as honesty, neatness, a good laugh. Now think of a few you don't like. Pick one from each list and create a character who embodies both.

Interview a character you want to develop. Be tough. Ask difficult and personal questions, insisting that the character be open and candid. Record the answers.

"A novelist is a person who lives in other people's skins." —E.L. Doctorow

CONVERSATION AND DIALOGUE

If you could have spoken at birth, what would you have said to your mother?
And she to you?

Jay Gatsby meets Emma Bovary on a moonlit night. Huck Finn goes sailing with Captain Ahab. What would they talk about? Create a conversation between two of your favorite characters from quite different novels.

"Always get to the dialogue as soon as possible. I always feel the thing to go for is speed. Nothing puts the reader off more than a great slab of prose at the start."

—P.G. Wodehouse

Eavesdrop on a co-worker's telephone conversation and record what she says. Compose a dialogue by inventing what was said by the person on the other end of the line.

Imagine meeting someone you loved years ago, who you've always wanted to see again but haven't heard from in years. What do you talk about? What _don't_ you talk about?

Listen to the people around you, noting their habits of speech—verbal tics, favorite words and phrases, mispronunciations. Use these quirks in a dialogue between characters.

On his car radio, Peter Schaffer heard about a local stable boy who went mad and blinded six horses. Schaffer quickly turned off the radio to avoid hearing the details; he wanted to imagine them. This led him to write "Equus," his famous play about an emotionally disturbed stable boy who believes that the horses in his care are constantly watching him.

Talk to a tree. What does it say to you?

Surely you've been in an argument and thought of the perfect comeback—two days too late. Well here's your chance. Re-create the argument as best you can, then add your response. What happens next?

"The theater is a communal event, like church. The playwright constructs a mass to be performed for a lot of people. She writes a prayer, which is just the longings of one heart." —Marsha Norman

What secrets does your pet keep from you? Reveal them from the animal's point of view.

Create a dialogue between yourself and the historical figure you'd most like to meet.

An animal rights activist sees a woman sporting a full-length lynx coat. The activist's first words are.... Continue this lively discussion.

"We write to taste life twice, in the moment and in retrospection." —Anaïs Nin

Write down three intriguing statements from different conversations you overhear today. Use them in a dialogue.

A close friend announces an important decision—a career change, a move across the country, a sudden engagement. You know this is a terrible mistake. How do you tell him without breaking his heart?

While hard at work on his classic poem "The Wasteland," T.S. Eliot began to insert lines verbatim from conversations with his gabby housemaid. Her Cockney accent and her gossip of the day fills much of the poem's pub scene, in which two drinkers chat away, ignoring the barman's call for closing time.

Take a trip into your past and record a conversation between who you are now and who you were then. What advice can you give the younger "you"?

Watch the television news. What do you think the anchors and the weather and sports reporters discuss during the five minutes before going on the air? Create the scene.

DESCRIPTIONS

Sit in a quiet room. Describe the silence.

Write about where you lived as a child. By describing the decorations in the home—paintings, photographs, furnishings—give a sense of what it was like to live there.

"You don't write about the horrors of war. No. You write about a kid's burnt socks lying in the road." —Richard Price

The bushes are mauve, the grass is fuchsia, the trees are turquoise. Keep the images coming and describe where in the world this might be.

Take your reader step by step through some process you do well—anything from making potato-leek soup to whittling a tent peg.

Tom Clancy was inspired to write his best-selling novel "The Hunt for Red October" by a newspaper article about a Russian frigate that made a wild break for Sweden to defect and was caught by the Russian navy. He turned the frigate into a high-tech submarine and began his novel of Cold War intrigue and suspense.

You're blind. You go to a public event—a concert, maybe, or a fair. Evoke it vividly, sensuously.

Get in your car or on a bus and drive for exactly one hour. Stop and describe where you are.

"Concentrate on what you want to say to yourself and your friends. Follow your inner moonlight; don't hide the madness. You say what you want to say when you don't care who's listening." —Allen Ginsberg

You are a pebble being churned into a tiny piece of sand by the ocean. How does this feel?

Stare up at the sky and depict what you see—clouds, stars, colors, birds, shafts of sunlight, lines of airplane exhaust. Add the thoughts and feelings these images inspire in you.

Capture the way something moves—a belly dancer, a snake in high grass, a carousel full of children on horses.

Share the emotions you felt when a friend let you down.

Leo Tolstoy caught the idea for the climax of his classic novel "Anna Karenina" from local gossip. He heard that his neighbor's mistress threw herself under an onrushing train when the affair ended. Anna Karenina, whose adultery does not lead to the happiness she'd hoped for, decides to kill herself in the same way.

Look closely at an object you rarely use—an electric drill, a food processor, a snow blower. Render it in exacting detail.

Gaze out your window. Report everything you see—trees, houses, people strolling past—as if you were from another planet.

We sometimes use colors to describe how we feel, such as when we're sad, we say we feel blue. Attach a color to your mood today. Are you purple? Orange? Why is this color appropriate?

"A poem is never a put-up job, so to speak. It begins as a lump in the throat, a sense of wrong, a homesickness, a lovesickness. It is never a thought to begin with."

—Robert Frost

Describe a moment of dizziness, how your perception changed for a few seconds.

OBSERVATIONS

You are a house plant. What do you think about the humans in your life—their habits, the way they live?

What are your co-workers talking about? Recent elections? Company procedures? Office romances? Discuss one key aspect of the subject they all seem to miss.

Finish this statement: The biggest difference between men and women is....
Now defend your view.

"I am a writer who came of a sheltered life. A sheltered life can be a daring life as well. For all serious daring starts within." —Eudora Welty

Borrow the opening of Truman Capote's "Breakfast at Tiffany's": "I'm always drawn back to places where I have lived. I am drawn to the houses and their neighborhoods." Then visit a neighborhood you used to live in and note the changes it has undergone—new buildings, homes where fields once were, new types of people.

What's your idea of heaven? How about hell?

Author Joan Didion was in a Las Vegas casino late one night when she heard a phone page for a struggling actress whose name she recognized. Didion watched as the actress, wearing a short white halter dress, walked through the casino toward the phone. Later, as she imagined who was paging the actress and why the actress was there, Didion began to write "Play It As It Lays," her novel of life on the Hollywood fringe.

Pick your favorite city—anywhere in the world. Why would you like to live there?

Write an argument against a cliche or truism. For example, explain that haste does not make waste or that sparing the rod doesn't spoil the child.

"Writing is really a way of thinking—not just feeling but thinking about things that are disparate, unresolved, mysterious, problematic or just sweet."

—Toni Morrison

Think of an issue you feel strongly about—one that gets you boiling. Write about it, taking the opposing view.

Carl Jung said, "Everything that irritates us about others can lead us to an understanding of ourselves." Write about a behavior that annoys you. What does this reaction say about you?

You are one hundred years old. Write about your first romance and then explain what you've learned of love over the years.

Sometimes writers flounder with a project because it's the wrong one. While blocked on a novel about vigilantes, John Steinbeck grew absorbed with the plight of migrant workers in his home state of California. He began taking time away from his novel to write news stories about them. Realizing that this was his true subject, he started a new novel, "The Grapes of Wrath," which changed the course of history.

Describe an airplane ride to your great-great-grandparents.

Do you have a "bad habit" that you can't seem to break? Instead of berating yourself, create a society in which this vice is a virtue, a land where smokers or nail-biters are revered.

Whip up a recipe for happiness. Be specific about the ingredients—marriage? money? travel? children?—and give the necessary proportions.

"In literature the ambition of the novice is to acquire the literary language; the struggle of the adept is to get rid of it." —George Bernard Shaw

You have the power to change the world. How _would_ you?

NAMES AND TITLES

Is there any question about the evil nature of Disney's Cruella Deville? Mordred of the King Arthur legend? Make a list of five knee-knocking names for the vilest of villains.

Kurt Vonnegut frequently chooses names for his characters from those on the mailboxes in his town. Take a drive and grab a few for yourself.

Think of a person who seems to fit his or her name perfectly. Why do you feel this way?

Revenge was sweet for Calder Willingham when he used a name to get back at poet Delmore Schwartz, who, while an editor at the "Partisan Review," rejected Willingham's work. In Willingham's novel "End as a Man," a whorehouse is named the Hotel Delmore. When someone told Schwartz about it, he said that Willingham probably had done this subconsciously. Willingham, however, crowed that the choice was very conscious indeed.

Flip through a road atlas and jot down interesting names of towns, cities, rivers, mountains. Pick a few that could also be used as names of characters.

Revenge was sweet for Calder Willingham when he used a name to get back at poet Delmore Schwartz, who, while an editor at the "Partisan Review," rejected Willingham's work. In Willingham's novel "End as a Man," a whorehouse is named the Hotel Delmore. When someone told Schwartz about it, he said that Willingham probably had done this subconsciously. Willingham, however, crowed that the choice was very conscious indeed.

Flip through a road atlas and jot down interesting names of towns, cities, rivers, mountains. Pick a few that could also be used as names of characters.

Play name association. List ten common first names, then write the initial impression that comes to mind.

"Read a lot and hit the streets. A writer who doesn't keep up with what's out there ain't gonna be out there." —Toni Cade Bambara

Give a character—yours or another writer's—a different name, one that suggests an entirely new identity. Would Sam Spade, for example, be quite so tough if he were Eugene Snerdly? How does your character change?

In his novel "The End of the Road," John Barth called his narrator Jacob Horner, a name he swiped form the nursery rhyme "Little Jack Horner." Grab a book of nursery rhymes and follow Barth's lead.

Think of three people or three of your characters who you know very well. Give each an appropriate or outrageous intimate pet name.

Pick a book from your shelves. Close your eyes, rifle through the pages and let your finger land anywhere. Use the word, phrase or sentence you're pointing to as a title.

"Almost all great writers have as their motif, more or less disguised, the passage from childhood to maturity, the clash between the thrill of expectation and the disillusioning knowledge of the truth. 'Lost Illusion' is the undisclosed title of every novel."

—André Maurois

Make a list of your five favorite books and think of a new title for each.

Writers sometimes try to write clever or tricky titles, but often the simplest are the best, such as Poe's "The Raven" or Chekhov's "Lady With the Pet Dog." Use the central images in some of your writing as titles.

Brainstorm fifteen titles for your manuscript. Now cross out each one. Which deletion hurt most?

Robert Heinlein only needed a title to launch into "The Door Into Summer," his famous novel of time travel. And he got one from his cat. On a winter day, the cat nosed at the door, as if wanting to go outside. But when Heinlein opened the door, the cat merely peered into the gray chill. After this happened a few times, Heinlein told his wife, who explained, "She's looking for a door into summer." He wrote down the title and began the novel.

Jot down a noun that describes the key emotion in a piece of writing you're working on. Now write a verb that embodies the main action. Use both words in the title.

Flip through a stack of magazines and pick a title that you like from the table of contents. Write a brief synopsis of a story or essay that might have such a title.

"If I feel physically as if the top of my head were taken off, I know that is poetry."

—Emily Dickinson

DREAMS AND ANECDOTES

You keep waking up in the middle of the same sexy dream. Too bad. Write the ending.

Describe a moment of déjà vu. What's it like to see your life pass before your eyes—again?

While sitting at his desk, unable to write, E.L. Doctorow began looking around the room and wondering about the original owners of his large Victorian home. His imaginings took him back to the turn of the century and led him to begin his best-selling novel "Ragtime," which is set in that era.

Have you ever dreamed you're somebody or something other than yourself?
Who or what are you?

Daydream yourself to a make-believe hideaway, then share it on paper.

In my wildest dreams I never imagined anything like this could happen to me....
Keep going.

"Seek those [themes] which your own everyday life offers you; describe your sorrows and desires, passing thoughts and the belief in some sort of beauty—describe all these with loving, quiet, humble sincerity, and use, to express yourself, the things in your environment, the images from your dreams, and the objects of your memory."

—Rainer Maria Rilke

Dreams often pair aspects of our lives that seem unconnected—such as umbrellas and cows. Write about how these parts _are_ connected. (Umbrellas and cows are waterproof, they're often seen outside, they can be black and white.)

Have you ever done something foolish or embarrassing in a dream? Pretend this really occurred. What happens next?

What stories about your family are often told when your relatives get together?

A typo in a newspaper article sparked Elizabeth Bishop's well-known poem "The Man-Moth." In the article, the "mammoth" appeared incorrectly as "manmoth." Bishop began to envision a mythic creature who was half-man, half-moth. The resulting poem chronicles the epic struggle of this beast, born of poor proofreading.

Recall a time when you told a lie—the more outrageous, the better. Explain what really happened, then how you bent the truth. Were you caught?

Write a scene in which a character tells a great story—but at the wrong time. The one about your mother forgetting her glasses and walking into the men's room might not be so hilarious during your first dinner with the new in-laws.

"If I didn't know the ending of a story, I wouldn't begin. I always write my last lines, my last paragraph, first, and then I go back and work towards it. I know where I'm going. I know what my goal is. And how I get there is God's grace."
—Katherine Anne Porter

What family event most changed your life? Your father losing his job? The birth of a brother? A move from Los Angeles to Boise?

List the names of several people you know. Next to each name, write an adjective or two that describes the person. Then recall and write a brief story involving the person to support your description.

Embellish an anecdote about yourself. Exaggerate the events and the reactions of the people involved—but keep a straight face. Don't let the reader sense that you're dressing things up a bit.

List the names of several people you know. Next to each name, write an adjective or two that describes the person. Then recall and write a brief story involving the person to support your description.

Embellish an anecdote about yourself. Exaggerate the events and the reactions of the people involved—but keep a straight face. Don't let the reader sense that you're dressing things up a bit.

"If you write a hundred short stories and they're all bad, that doesn't mean you've failed. You only fail if you stop writing." —Ray Bradbury

More From Story Press!

Turning Life Into Fiction, by Robin Hemley. Writers' lives, those of their friends and family members, newspaper accounts, conversations overheard—these can be the bases for novels and short stories. Here, Robin Hemley shows how to make true stories even better. You'll learn how to turn journal entries into fiction; find good story material within yourself; identify memories that can be developed; and fictionalize other people's stories. Exercises guide writers in honing their skills. #48000/$17.99/208 pages

The Joy of Writing Sex, by Elizabeth Benedict. Finally, here's the book to help you craft intimate scenes that are original, sensitive and just right for your fiction. Elizabeth Benedict's instruction, supported with examples from the finest contemporary fiction, focuses on creating sensual encounters that hinge on freshness of character, dialogue, mood and plot. You'll also find spirited opinions from some of today's most prestigious writers—among them, John Updike, Dorothy Allison, Russell Banks and Joyce Carol Oates. #48021/$16.99/160 pages

The ABC's of Writing Fiction, by Ann Copeland. With a teaching style that's dynamic and offbeat, Ann Copeland offers an authoritative wealth of instruction, advice and insight on the writing life. Penetrating alphabetical mini-lessons and unexpected words and phrases—culled from 15 years of teaching fiction—encourage browsing, free associating and random discoveries. #48017/$18.99/256 pages

Fiction Writer's Workshop, by Josip Novakovich. In this interactive workshop, you'll explore each aspect of the art of fiction including point of view, description, revision, voice and more. At the end of each chapter you'll find more than a dozen writing exercises to help you put what you've learned into action. #48003/$17.99/256 pages

The Fiction Dictionary, by Laurie Henry. The essential guide to the inside language of fiction. These are terms from yesterday, today—and even those just being coined for the language of tomorrow. Some you've heard of; others may open up exciting new possibilities in your own writing. You'll discover genres you've never explored, writing devices you'll want to attempt, fresh characters to populate your stories. *The Fiction Dictionary* dusts off the traditional concept of "dictionary" by giving full, vivid descriptions, and by using lively examples from classic and contemporary fiction . . . turning an authoritative reference into a can't-put-it-down browser. #48008/$18.99/336 pages

The Poetry Dictionary, by John Drury. This comprehensive book unravels the rich and complex language of poetry with clear, working definitions. Drury's discussions of poetic forms, elements, tools and traditions result in a volume that is the definitive source for today's poet. In many cases, several different poems are used to illustrate the many ways poets have put theories to work, making *The Poetry Dictionary* a unique anthology. #48007/$18.99/336 pages

Creative Nonfiction, by Philip Gerard. Nonfiction is in the facts. Creative nonfiction is in the telling. With this engaging book, you'll learn how to tell a story with power and grace to create compelling, unforgettable pieces. Philip Gerard's clear and passionate instruction covers every step of the writing process—from finding an original subject to conducting a stirring interview to working with an editor. Plus, you'll get the opportunity to follow in his footsteps as he shows you, step-by-step, how one of his own pieces came together. #48016/$17.99/224 pages

The Best Writing on Writing, edited by Jack Heffron, is the first in a series that will showcase the most provocative new articles, essays and lectures on fiction, nonfiction, poetry, playwriting and the writing life. These 27 illuminating and thought-provoking selections are a lively feast of the well-written word and how it is fashioned. #48001/$16.99/208 pages/paperback

The Best Writing on Writing, Volume 2, edited by Jack Heffron, is the year's best collection of memorable essays, book excerpts and lectures on fiction, nonfiction, poetry, screenwriting and the writing life, all from 1994. The selections feature such luminaries as Joyce Carol Oates, Margaret Atwood, Justin Kaplan, Charles Baxter and Maxine Kumin to name a few. #48013/$16.99/224 pages/paperback